Imagine! 6

Oxford Read and Imagine

The Secret on the Moon

By Paul Shipton

Illustrated by Carl Pearce

Activities by Hannah Fish

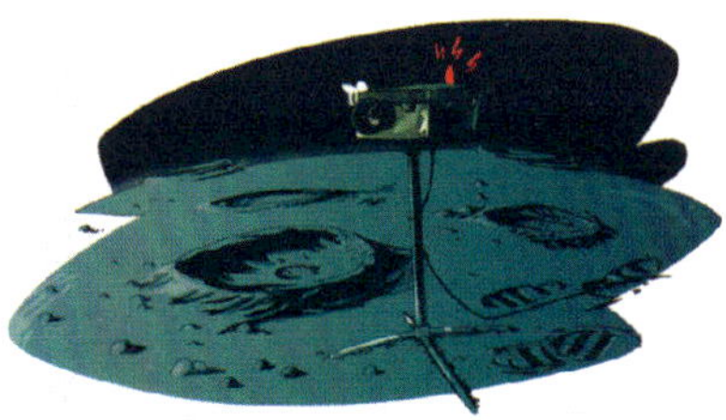

Contents

- Meet the Characters 2
- The Secret on the Moon 4
- Activities 36
- Project 52
- Glossary 54
- About Read and Imagine. 56
- Key (Activities for Exam Practice). 56

OXFORD
UNIVERSITY PRESS

Meet the Characters

Ben and Rosie are always ready for a new adventure in Grandpa's amazing van.

The van can fly. It can change shape. It can go anywhere in the world in moments … And it can travel through time!

Ben and Rosie are ready for their next adventure. Are *you*?

Grandpa Ben and Rosie's grandfather, a scientist and inventor

Clunk Grandpa's robot

Ben Rosie's brother

Rosie Ben's sister

Alice Rosie's friend

Tom an astronaut who flies to the Moon

Mike another astronaut

Years ago, two astronauts landed on the Moon. But, they found that they were not alone. Who was hiding and watching them?

Read *The Secret on the Moon* and find out.

Chapter One

'Ben, what are you doing?' asked Rosie.

Ben looked up from his work. 'I have to do some homework,' he said. 'We're learning about the Moon in class.'

Rosie's friend Alice pointed at one of the photos on Ben's computer. It showed an astronaut on the surface of the Moon.

'Just think …' said Alice. 'How did the astronauts feel when they stood on the Moon?'

Ben smiled. 'I've been looking at a website about that,' he said. 'Some people think that astronauts *never* landed on the Moon. They say that the photos were taken on Earth!'

‘*What?*’ Grandpa was at the door. ‘When astronauts landed on the Moon, it was a very important moment in history!’ he said. ‘People should be proud of it!’

Grandpa turned. ‘Clunk!’ he shouted. ‘Come here, please!’

The little robot appeared. ‘Yes?’ he asked. ‘I was watching TV.’

‘There’s no time for that,’ said Grandpa. ‘I want you to take Ben, Rosie, and Alice on a trip. I want you to take them to the Moon!’

‘Brilliant!’ said Ben and Rosie.

Alice smiled, but she looked worried.

Go to page 36 for activities.

As the children were leaving, Grandpa spoke quietly to Clunk. 'I can't come with you on this trip,' he said. 'But there's something very important that you'll have to do …'

Five minutes later, the children were all waiting in the van.

'Are you ready?' asked Clunk.

'YES!'

Clunk started the van and suddenly there were bright lights all around them. The lights went round and round, faster and faster, and then a tunnel appeared in the middle. Clunk drove the van straight into that tunnel. WHOOSH!

Seconds later, the van flew out the other end …

'We're in space!' said Rosie.

Ben looked out the window. 'We've never been so far from Earth. Or so close to the Moon!'

They could see the many craters on the Moon's surface from here.

'We haven't just traveled in space,' said Clunk. 'We've traveled in *time*, too!'

'Are we in the future?' asked Alice.

'No,' said Clunk. 'We've gone back into the past – to the time of one of the early landings on the Moon. Grandpa wants you to see it!'

Go to page 37 for activities.

Chapter Two

A few minutes later, the van was on the Moon.

'It's so empty here,' said Alice.

Ben agreed. The surface of the Moon was as empty as a desert, with only gray dust and rocks and the darkness of space above.

'Do you want to go outside?' Clunk asked. 'We have two spacesuits in the van.'

'Only two?' said Ben.

'That's OK,' said Alice nervously. 'I'd prefer to stay in the van.'

When Ben and Rosie were wearing the spacesuits, they moved to the back of the van. One door closed behind them, and a second door opened in front of them.

It was time to walk on the Moon.

'This is an amazing moment,' said Ben on the radio in his helmet. 'We should say something important.'

'You're right,' said Rosie and she jumped onto the Moon. '*Let's go!*'

'Don't go too far,' Clunk told them on the radio. 'The astronauts are going to land soon. They mustn't see us.'

→ Go to page 38 for activities.

'Why not?' asked Rosie.

'If the astronauts see us here on the Moon, it will change history,' answered Ben.

'Is that bad?' asked Rosie.

'Yes,' said Ben. 'Terrible! If we change something important in the past, it might change *everything* in our time.'

'Don't worry,' said Clunk on the radio. 'They won't see us if we stay here.'

Rosie began to play and jump around. 'This is fun!' she said. She jumped up very high. 'Wow!'

'Gravity on the Moon's much weaker than on Earth,' Ben laughed. 'You can jump six times higher!'

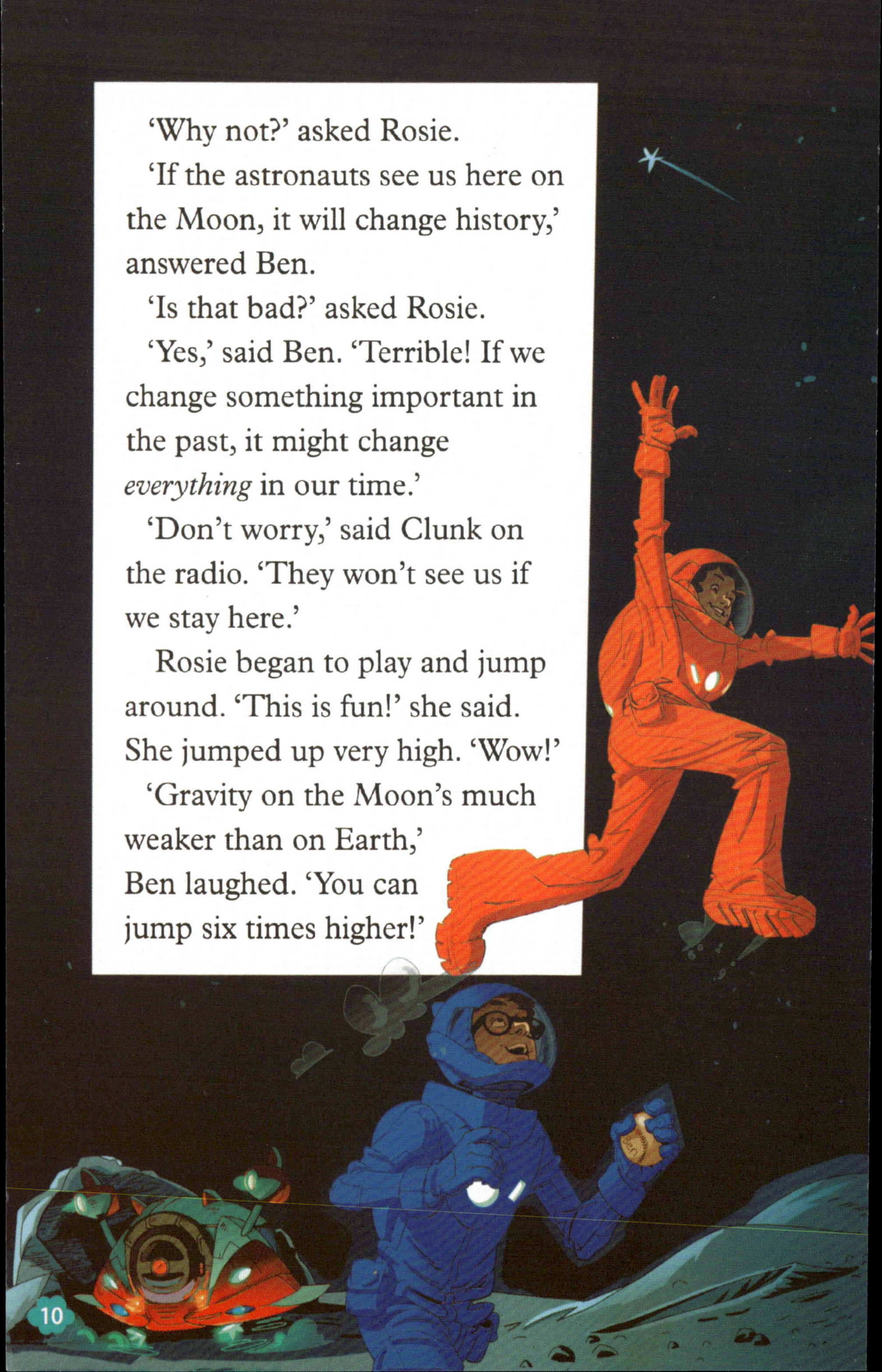

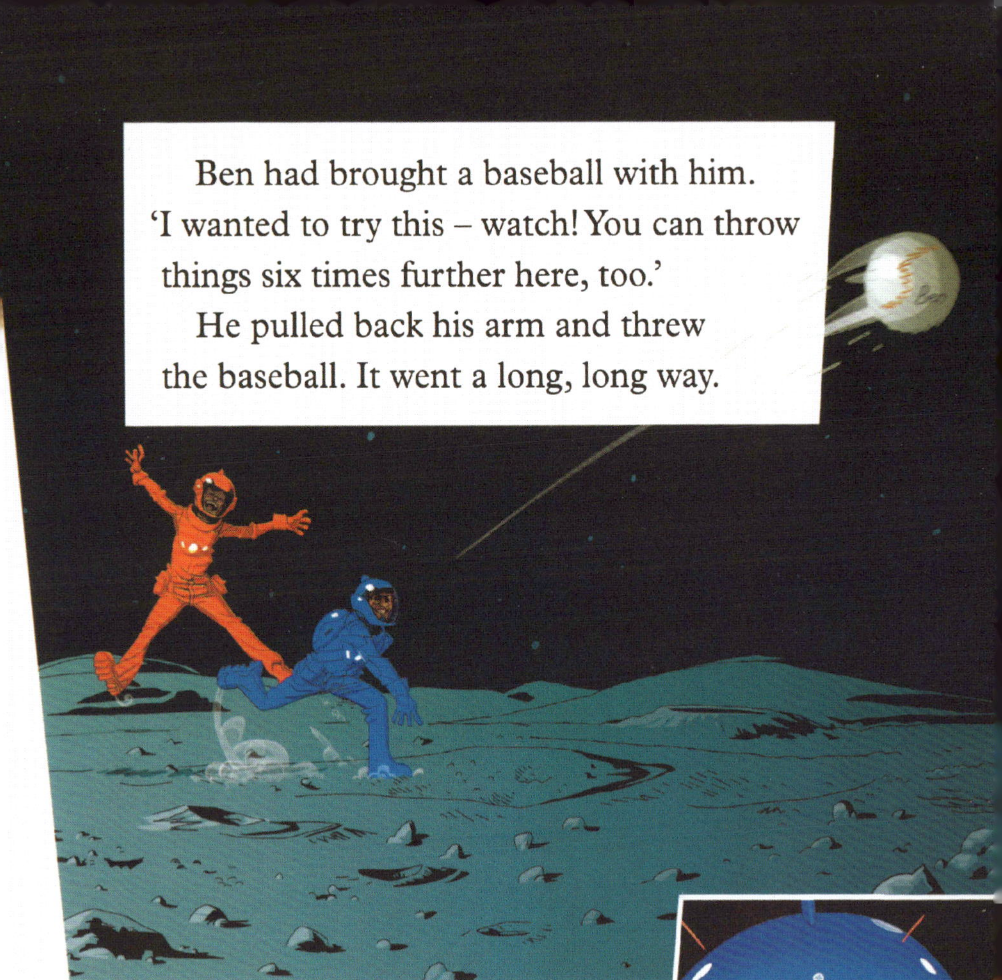

Ben had brought a baseball with him. 'I wanted to try this – watch! You can throw things six times further here, too.'

He pulled back his arm and threw the baseball. It went a long, long way.

'I've never thrown anything so far in my life,' said Ben proudly.

But Rosie was worried. 'Wait,' she said. 'Where did Clunk say that the astronauts are going to land?'

Ben's smile disappeared. 'Oh no,' he said. 'I threw the ball in that direction. What if the first astronauts ever on this part of the Moon find a baseball with my name on it?'

Go to page 39 for activities.

Chapter Three

Ben started to move in the direction of the baseball. He couldn't run easily, so he had to move by jumping.

'I must get that ball before the astronauts arrive,' he said.

'Wait,' said Rosie. 'I'll come with you.'

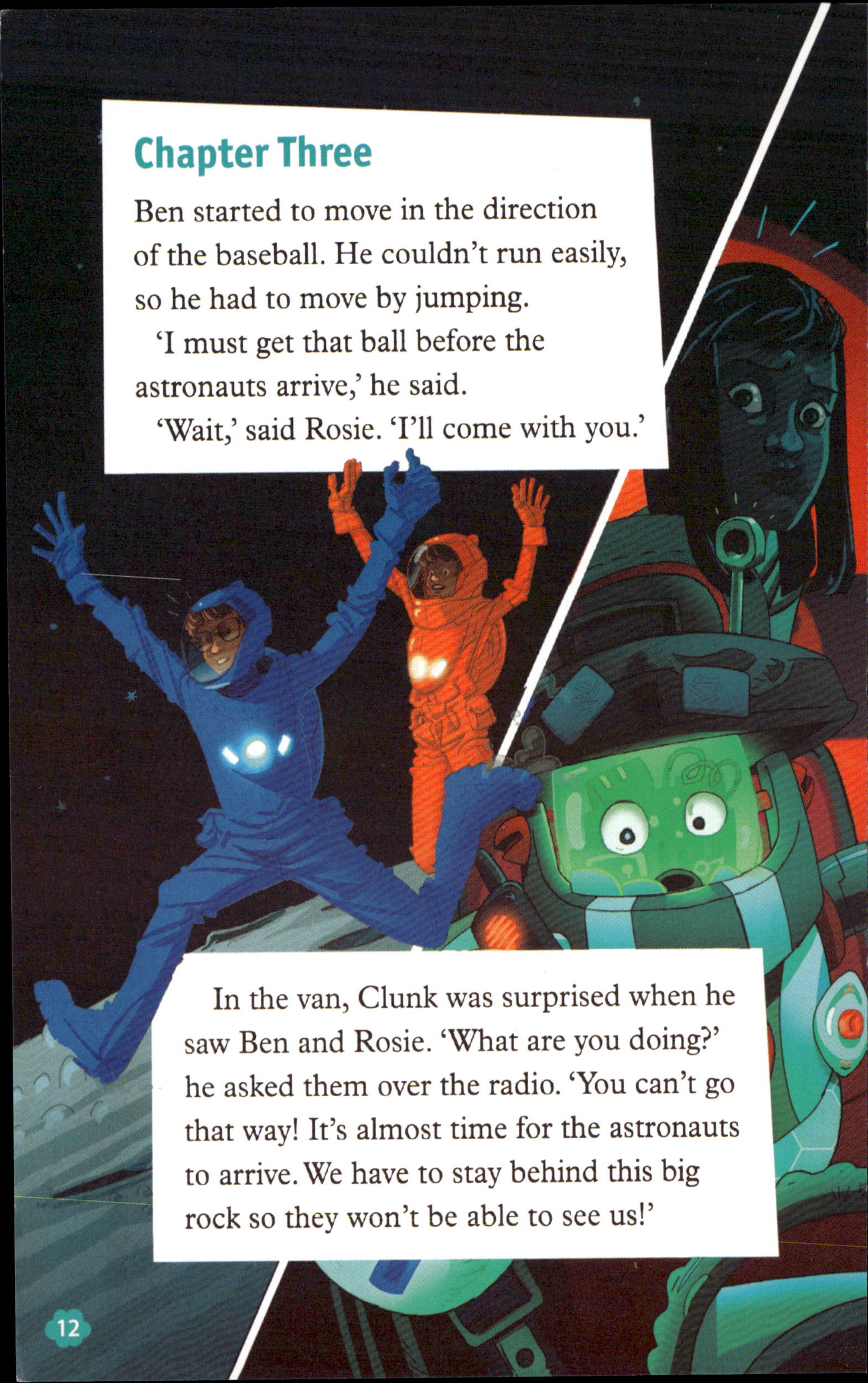

In the van, Clunk was surprised when he saw Ben and Rosie. 'What are you doing?' he asked them over the radio. 'You can't go that way! It's almost time for the astronauts to arrive. We have to stay behind this big rock so they won't be able to see us!'

Ben quickly explained the problem to Clunk.

'We should use the van to get Ben and Rosie *and* the baseball,' said Alice. 'That's probably the quickest way.'

But before Clunk could start the van, there was a flash of light in the darkness of space above them.

'We're too late!' said Clunk. 'That light is the astronauts' landing vehicle. It's flying down to the surface while the bigger part of the rocket orbits the Moon.'

The light got bigger and bigger. The landing vehicle was coming closer.

Go to page 40 for activities.

'Ben and Rosie!' said Clunk into the radio. 'You mustn't let the astronauts see you. They have a camera that sends pictures down to Earth. If they see you here on the Moon, millions of people on Earth will see you, too!'

Ben and Rosie could also see the light of the landing vehicle. There was no time for them to go back to the van.

'What can we do?' asked Rosie.

'Here!' said Ben. He jumped into a small crater. 'We can hide in here!'

'What now?' asked Rosie.

'We'll just have to wait,' said Ben.

He put his head out of the crater a little.

The landing vehicle was coming down, lower and lower. Clouds of dust from the Moon went up. At last the landing vehicle landed – it was on the Moon.

Ben knew that he was watching an important moment in history, but he couldn't enjoy it. There were two big scary questions in his mind …

Were the astronauts going to find the baseball?

And if they found it, what would happen then?

Go to page 41 for activities.

Chapter Four

A door on the landing vehicle opened.

'There's a camera on that door,' Ben told his sister. 'It's going to film the first astronaut when he leaves the vehicle.'

A few moments later, an astronaut appeared and began to climb slowly down the ladder. When the astronaut was on the Moon, he put a second camera in front of the vehicle.

'Pictures from that camera are being sent to a satellite, and then to TVs all around the world,' Ben told Rosie.

The second astronaut came down the ladder.

After a few minutes, the two astronauts began to collect dust and small rocks.

'They're going to take those home to Earth for scientists to study,' explained Ben.

Ben and Rosie watched for a long time.

'They can't stay out of the landing vehicle for much longer,' said Ben. 'Those old spacesuits don't have a lot of air.'

'Maybe they won't see the baseball,' said Rosie.

Hope began to grow inside Ben when one of the two astronauts started to climb back up the ladder.

But the other astronaut didn't follow him. He was looking at something to one side of the vehicle.

Go to page 42 for activities.

'Clunk! What shall we do?' asked Ben over the radio. 'They're going to see the ball.'

Before Clunk could answer, Grandpa's face appeared on the computer screen in front of him. 'Clunk, I've recorded this message for you. You must do everything that I tell you.'

'What's happening?' said Alice.

'I'm not sure,' said Clunk.

'You must leave Ben and Rosie here and take the van to Earth right now,' said Grandpa. 'Listen very carefully ...'

'We can't leave Rosie and Ben here!' shouted Alice.

But Clunk had started the van and they were already leaving.

'Clunk! Where are you going?' Rosie said into her radio. There was no answer.

Rosie was starting to feel afraid. Ben was afraid, too.

The astronaut was moving closer to the baseball. He was probably asking himself why this rock was much rounder than all the others.

Then he stopped. He could see now that this wasn't a Moon rock.

He reached down carefully and picked the ball up. He held it in his hand and studied it.

Ben watched nervously. What was the astronaut thinking now?

Go to page 43 for activities.

Chapter Five

The astronaut, whose name was Tom, looked at the baseball in his hand for a long time.

Tom had trained for years. He had dreamed of walking on the Moon. He had thought that he was ready for anything.

He was wrong.

The name BEN was written on the baseball in blue ink.

'How?' Tom thought. 'How could there be a baseball *here*?'

Was this really happening? Was he dreaming?

Tom felt suddenly afraid and far from home. It was harder and harder for him to breathe. He turned and started to run back to the landing vehicle.

As Tom ran, he forgot to look down. One of his feet hit a rock and he fell.

Ben and Rosie watched nervously.

'Is he OK?' asked Rosie. 'He isn't getting up.'

Ben said nothing. Had the astronaut hit his head inside his helmet? Or maybe there wasn't enough air in his spacesuit now?

'Won't the other astronaut come out and look for him?' asked Rosie.

'He can't,' said Ben. 'Those old spacesuits don't have enough air. *We* have to help him. If we don't, he might die.'

But if they helped him, millions of people on Earth would see them …

Go to page 44 for activities.

Clunk and Alice were still in the van.

'Why have we come back to Earth?' asked Alice. 'We have to go back to the Moon and get Ben and Rosie!'

The van had arrived outside a small house in the countryside. Behind the house there was a small shed.

'Don't worry, Alice,' Clunk said. 'Grandpa explained what we have to do.'

He knocked on the shed door.

A tall teenager with big glasses opened the door.

'Hello, Richard,' said Clunk. 'Please don't be afraid.'

The teenager looked more amazed than afraid.

'A robot?' he said. 'How wonderful!'

Richard smiled. 'Can I look inside your head?' he asked Clunk excitedly. 'I'm very interested in robots.'

'There's no time,' said Clunk. 'What do you know about the Moon landing?'

'Everything!' said Richard. He pointed to a black-and-white TV inside the shed. 'I've been watching it while I work.'

'We need your help,' said Clunk. He told the teenager what he wanted him to do.

'I can't do that!' said Richard.

'If you don't, one of those astronauts is going to die,' said Alice.

'OK,' said Richard immediately. 'I'll help.'

→ Go to page 45 for activities.

Chapter Six

Richard worked quickly. Soon he'd built a new machine from the many parts in his shed.

'This will stop the signal from the Moon,' he said. 'Nobody will see what's happening there for about ten minutes. Is that long enough?'

'I hope so,' said Alice.

Richard turned on the machine.

All around the world, people were watching live pictures from the Moon. They'd seen one astronaut as he returned to the landing vehicle.

But where was the second astronaut?

Suddenly the pictures stopped.

Everywhere people were asking the same question: 'What happened?'

On the Moon, Ben and Rosie had reached the astronaut. Ben put his hands under the man's arms. 'You take his feet,' he told Rosie. 'We'll have to carry him.'

'What about the camera?' asked Rosie.

Then she noticed something. The camera's red light was off.

'Look, Ben,' she said. 'I don't think that the camera's sending any pictures to Earth now.'

'Perhaps Clunk did something to it!' said Ben.

Slowly, they carried the astronaut to the landing vehicle.

'What now?' asked Rosie.

Ben thought about this. 'We should knock on the door!'

Go to page 46 for activities.

A few minutes later, the children and the two astronauts were inside the landing vehicle.

'I can't believe this,' said the second astronaut, whose name was Mike. He looked confused and afraid.

Tom was starting to open his eyes. 'Are … are you really here?' he asked when he saw the two children.

'They're real,' said Mike. 'And they saved your life, Tom.'

'I don't understand any of this,' said Tom. He looked at Ben and Rosie. 'But thank you.'

'Now please explain why and how you're here,' said Mike.

Grandpa had always told the children not to tell anybody about the van. But Ben knew that he couldn't lie to these astronauts.

'We've come from the future,' he said.

'What?' Tom and Mike looked surprised. 'Can everybody in the future travel back in time?' Tom asked.

'No,' laughed Rosie. 'Only our Grandpa!' She quickly explained how they had come to the Moon.

Tom listened carefully. Then he said, 'People on Earth call Mike and me brave because we came to the Moon. But you two young people are just as brave as we are.'

Go to page 47 for activities.

Chapter Seven

Alice nervously looked from the black TV screen to Richard's machine and back again. The ten minutes were almost over.

'What's happening on the Moon?' she thought. 'Will I ever see my friends again?'

Suddenly there was a loud sound from outside. A helicopter was landing!

Clunk moved to the door. 'We have to leave before anyone sees us.'

But it was too late. The shed door opened and a tall man with glasses was looking at them.

'Nobody is going anywhere until I know what's happening,' he said.

The man's name was Professor Muller, and he was the head of the space program.

'When the signal from the Moon stopped, we looked for the problem,' he said. 'We found out that it was coming from this place.'

Alice, Clunk, and Richard knew that they could not lie. They explained everything. They were amazed that Professor Muller believed them.

'Nobody else can ever know about this,' Muller said.

'Am I in trouble?' asked Richard.

'No.' Muller smiled. 'You're a brilliant young man. I want to give you a job in the space program.'

Go to page 48 for activities.

On the Moon, Ben gave the baseball to Tom. 'Keep this to remember us,' he said.

Tom's last words to them were, 'Goodbye, and good luck!'

Then, Ben and Rosie went outside the landing vehicle again.

Seconds after the children walked away from the landing vehicle, the camera's red light came on again.

Soon it was time for the landing vehicle to take off. It was the start of the astronauts' long journey back to Earth.

Ben and Rosie watched as the vehicle grew smaller and smaller.

But where were Clunk and Alice? Where was the van? Ben and Rosie were alone.

The Moon moved through space, and suddenly they saw the Earth. It was a beautiful, blue ball in the darkness of space.

Earth looked so different from the dead, gray rock of the Moon. Ben and Rosie knew that it was full of life, with plants and animals, seas and woods, rain and snow and lovely blue skies. And there were people, millions of them – cities and towns full of people.

'I want to go home,' said Rosie.

'Me, too,' said Ben quietly.

Go to page 49 for activities.

Chapter Eight

Ben didn't know how long they'd sat there. He was getting more and more worried. How much air did they have in their spacesuits now?

If Clunk didn't come back soon, this trip was going to become very dangerous.

Suddenly, Rosie said, 'What's that?'

Something far away was moving across the surface of the Moon. Its colors were bright and beautiful in this dead, gray place.

It was Grandpa's van, and it was coming to get them! Soon they could see Clunk and Alice's faces inside the van.

'We're going home!' said Rosie happily.

When they arrived back outside their house, Ben and Rosie looked around at the sky above them, and the green grass under their feet. Birds were singing, and they could feel the wind on their faces. It felt wonderful.

'Earth!' said Rosie. 'What a fantastic place!'

A face appeared at the open window. It was Grandpa. He looked happy to see the children. 'Quick,' he said. 'Come inside. There's someone that I want you to meet. He's an old friend.'

Go to page 50 for activities.

An old man was sitting inside. His hair was gray and there were lines on his face, but Ben and Rosie recognized him immediately. It was Tom the astronaut.

'I've waited many years to see you again,' he told Ben and Rosie. 'When Mike and I came home, Professor Muller talked to us. He asked us never to tell anybody about you. Nobody else ever knew what really happened on the Moon that day. It's been our secret all these years.'

He pulled something from his pocket and smiled. 'This is yours, Ben. I've had it for a long, long time.'

It was the baseball.

Alice was looking at a photo on the wall. It showed Grandpa when he was a young man. He was standing with a taller man who wore glasses – Professor Muller.

'Wait a minute,' said Alice. 'One other person knew about what happened … Richard.' She turned to Grandpa. 'Were you the teenager who helped us?'

'Yes.' Grandpa smiled. 'That's why I didn't come on this trip. I didn't want to change history by meeting myself in the past!'

Ben was standing at the window. 'Look,' he said. 'The Moon's beautiful this evening.'

Go to page 51 for activities.

Activities for pages 4–5

PET

1 Find and write the words.

1 how you feel when you have done something well — p r o u d
2 where we all live — E _ _ _ _
3 to suddenly be seen — a _ _ _ _ _
4 a person who goes into space — a _ _ _ _ _ _ _ _
5 the outer part of something — s _ _ _ _ _ _
6 to come down to the ground — l _ _ _

2 Circle the mistakes. Then write the correct words.

1 Ben was learning about the Earth in class. Moon
2 They looked at a painting of an astronaut on the Moon. ______
3 Ben had looked at a book about the Moon. ______
4 Some people think astronauts always landed on the Moon. ______
5 They think the photos were taken on airplanes. ______
6 Grandpa asked Dad to take the children to the Moon. ______
7 Ben and Rosie were excited, but Alice looked happy. ______

Talk **Do you think astronauts landed on the Moon? Tell a friend your ideas.**

Activities for pages 6–7

1 Read the sentences. Choose and write the correct words.

1 Grandpa couldn't ___come___ on this trip.

a coming **b** came ~~**c** come~~

2 There was an important job for Clunk ________ do.

a to **b** will **c** can

3 Clunk started the van and bright lights ________.

a appearing **b** appear **c** appeared

4 Clunk and the children were ________ space!

a at **b** in **c** on

5 They were very far ________ Earth.

a to **b** from **c** off

6 They could see craters on the ________ surface.

a Moon's **b** its **c** Moons

7 They ________ traveling in space and time.

a had **b** were **c** been

8 They traveled back into ________ past.

a the **b** a **c** that

Talk **Would you like to go to the Moon? Talk to a friend.**

Activities for pages 8–9

PET

1 Choose the correct answers.

1 What was the surface of the Moon like?

a It was as dark as space.

b It was empty.

c It looked just like Earth.

d It looked like a big tunnel.

2 Why did Alice want to stay in the van?

a because she wanted to help Clunk

b because she was nervous

c because she wanted to drive the van

d because she was tired

3 Why did Ben think they should say something important?

a to check that Clunk could hear them

b because he had a radio on his helmet

c to find out if there were people on the Moon

d because it was an amazing moment

4 Why couldn't Ben and Rosie go too far?

a because the astronauts were landing soon

b because they could get lost

c because Clunk needed to speak to them

d because the astronauts needed to see them

Activities for pages 10–11

1 Decide if the sentences are *correct* (A) or *incorrect* (B).

1	If the astronauts saw them, it could change history.	A	B
2	It would be fine if the astronauts saw them.	A	B
3	Rosie started to play on the Moon.	A	B
4	Rosie couldn't jump very high on the Moon.	A	B
5	Gravity on the Moon is weaker than on Earth.	A	B
6	You can jump six times higher on the Moon.	A	B
7	Ben had a baseball with him.	A	B
8	Ben kicked the baseball and it went a long way.	A	B
9	The ball went to where the astronauts would land.	A	B
10	The baseball had Rosie's name on it.	A	B

2 Match.

Earth

Moon

- 1 stronger gravity
- 2 craters
- 3 houses
- 4 empty
- 5 busy
- 6 weaker gravity

Activities for pages 12–13

1 Order the events.

Rosie went with Ben. ____

There was a flash of light in the darkness. ____

The landing vehicle came closer. ____

Ben started to move toward the baseball. __1__

Ben explained the problem to Clunk. ____

Clunk spoke to Ben and Rosie on his radio. ____

2 Match. Then write the sentences.

1 Ben had to move	the astronauts to arrive.
2 He had to get the ball	light above them.
3 It was almost time for	before the astronauts arrived.
4 Clunk wanted them	by jumping.
5 There was a flash of	astronauts' landing vehicle.
6 The light was the	to stay behind the rock.

1 Ben had to move by jumping.

2 ____________________

3 ____________________

4 ____________________

5 ____________________

6 ____________________

Activities for pages 14–15

PET

1 Choose and write the correct words.

Ben and Rosie could [1] ___see___ the light of the landing vehicle. They jumped [2] ________ a crater to hide. Ben put [3] ________ head out of the crater. He could see the landing vehicle. It was coming down [4] ________ . Clouds of dust [5] ________ the Moon went up. Then it [6] ________ on the Moon. Ben was watching an [7] ________ moment in history. But he couldn't enjoy it. He was too scared. Ben was worried about the baseball, and what [8] ________ happen if the astronauts found it.

1 **a** saw **(b)** see **c** seeing **d** seen

2 **a** onto **b** up to **c** into **d** at

3 **a** he's **b** he **c** him **d** his

4 **a** bottom **b** below **c** under **d** lower

5 **a** from **b** at **c** of **d** to

6 **a** landing **b** landed **c** was landed **d** land

7 **a** importantly **b** importance **c** important **d** import

8 **a** will **b** going to **c** would **d** would've

Activities for pages 16–17

KET

1 Find and write the words.

1 something that orbits the Earth s_ _ _ _ _ _ _ _

2 to take moving pictures using a camera f_ _ _

3 you can climb up and down this l_ _ _ _ _

4 astronauts wear one of these s_ _ _ _ _ _ _ _

2 Look at the picture on page 17 and write *yes* or *no*.

1 There are two astronauts on the landing vehicle. no

2 The landing vehicle is gray and black. ______

3 There is one astronaut on the ladder of the landing vehicle. ______

4 The astronaut on the ladder is holding a baseball. ______

5 The astronaut on the ladder is wearing white space suit and white boots. ______

6 The surface of the Moon is gray and rocky. ______

7 There is a big crater on the surface of the Moon. ______

8 In the sky, there are stars. ______

Talk **What was the astronaut was looking at? Tell a friend your ideas.**

Activities for pages 18–19

PET

1 Choose the best answers.

1 Rosie: Can you see the astronaut?

Ben: b

2 Rosie: What is he looking at?

Ben: ___

3 Rosie: What is he doing now?

Ben: ___

4 Rosie: Oh no! What should we do?

Ben: ___

5 Rosie: Yes, he might be able to help us.

Ben: ___

a Use your radio to tell Clunk.

b Yes, he's looking at something.

c I think it's the astronaut.

d He's picking it up!

e I hope so!

f I think it's the baseball.

g I don't think so!

h What do you think?

Talk **What happens next? Tell a friend your ideas.**

Activities for pages 20–21

1 Circle the mistakes. Then write the correct words.

1 Tom looked for the baseball in his hand. ____________

2 Tom had dreaming of walking on the Moon. ____________

3 Tom felt afraid and far for home. ____________

4 He started to ran back to the landing vehicle. ____________

5 But Tom forgot for look down. ____________

6 Tom's foot hit a rock and he falls. ____________

2 Circle the correct answers.

1 How long had Tom trained for?

months days years

2 What was written on the baseball?

Tom Ben Rosie

3 Why did Tom run back to the landing vehicle?

he felt afraid he wanted the baseball he was dreaming

4 What could happen if Ben and Rosie don't help Tom?

he could get up he could get help he could die

5 What would happen if they do help Tom?

he would have air he would die people would see them

Activities for pages 22–23

KET

1 Choose the correct answers.

1 Clunk and Alice were back on Earth.

(a Right) b Wrong c Doesn't say

2 Alice was angry with Clunk for taking them back.

a Right b Wrong c Doesn't say

3 They were at a house in the countryside.

a Right b Wrong c Doesn't say

4 Behind the house there was a big shed.

a Right b Wrong c Doesn't say

5 A teenager called Richard opened the shed door.

a Right b Wrong c Doesn't say

6 Alice smiled at Richard when he opened the door.

a Right b Wrong c Doesn't say

7 Richard wasn't very interested in robots.

a Right b Wrong c Doesn't say

8 Richard said he would help them.

a Right b Wrong c Doesn't say

Talk **What does Clunk want Richard to do?**

Tell a friend your ideas.

Activities for pages 24–25

1 Who said this? Write the names.

1 'What about the camera?' Rosie
2 'We should knock on the door!' ______
3 'This will stop the signal from the Moon.' ______
4 'What happened?' ______
5 'We'll have to carry him.' ______

2 Match. Then write the sentences.

1 Richard built a machine	for about ten minutes.
2 The machine stopped the	astronaut to the landing vehicle.
3 It stopped the signal	from the parts in the shed.
4 Ben and Rosie carried the	knocked on the door.
5 Ben and Rosie	signal from the Moon.

1 ______
2 ______
3 ______
4 ______
5 ______

Activities for pages 26–27

1 Choose and write the correct words.

Ben and Rosie were now [1] __________ the landing vehicle. The second astronaut was [2] __________ Mike, and he looked [3] __________. When Tom opened his eyes, he was confused, [4] __________. Mike and Tom wanted to [5] __________ how and why Ben and Rosie [6] __________ on the Moon. Ben explained that they had [7] __________ from the future [8] __________ Grandpa's van. Mike and Tom were very surprised. Tom said that Ben and Rosie were very [9] __________.

1 **a** on **b** to **c** inside **d** of

2 **a** name **b** call **c** calling **d** called

3 **a** confused **b** confusing **c** confuse **d** to confuse

4 **a** to **b** too **c** two **d** as too

5 **a** knew **b** knows **c** know **d** knowing

6 **a** had **b** went **c** saw **d** were

7 **a** coming **b** came **c** come d were

8 **a** on **b** in **c** at **d** from

9 **a** brave **b** bravely **c** bravest **d** braver

PET

Activities for pages 28–29

PET

1 Choose the correct answers.

1 Why was Alice looking nervously at the TV screen?

- **a** because Richard's machine wasn't working
- **b** because Richard had gone out of the shed
- **c** because the ten minutes were almost over
- **d** because she couldn't find Clunk

2 What was the sound from outside?

- **a** It was Clunk at the door.
- **b** It was a helicopter landing.
- **c** It was Grandpa's van.
- **d** It was Richard's machine breaking.

3 Who was in the helicopter?

- **a** Ben and Rosie
- **b** Mike and Tom
- **c** Professor Muller
- **d** two men from the space program

4 Why was Professor Muller at the shed?

- **a** because he wanted to give Alice a job
- **b** because he wanted to find Clunk
- **c** because he knew they had stopped the signal from the Moon
- **d** because he was the head of the space program

Activities for pages 30–31

1 Read the sentences. Choose and write the correct words.

1 Ben and Rosie watched the landing vehicle __________ off.

a get **b** go **c** take

2 The astronauts had a __________ journey back to Earth.

a long **b** far **c** tall

3 Suddenly Ben and Rosie __________ Earth.

a had seen **b** have seen **c** saw

4 Earth looked __________ a beautiful, blue ball.

a like **b** as **c** to

5 Ben and Rosie wanted __________ go home.

a for **b** to **c** that

2 Match.

1 Ben gave the •	• landing vehicle grow smaller.
2 The camera's red •	• on the Moon.
3 Ben and Rosie watched the •	• Clunk and Alice were.
4 Now they were alone •	• baseball to Tom.
5 They didn't where •	• light came on again.

KET

Activities for pages 32–33

1 Circle the correct words.

1 On the Moon, Ben was getting **brave** / **worried**.

2 He didn't know how much **air** / **life** they had in their spacesuits.

3 Suddenly, they saw Grandpa's **face** / **van**.

4 When they arrived at their house, it felt **wonderful** / **terrible**.

5 Grandpa was very **worried** / **happy** to see the children.

6 There was someone that Grandpa wanted them to **meet** / **find**.

2 Look at the picture on page 33 and write *yes* or *no*.

1 There are four children and one robot. ________

2 Clunk is sitting in the front of the van. ________

3 Alice is in the van. ________

4 Rosie is wearing red shoes. ________

5 The van is parked outside a house. ________

6 There are trees and flowers around the house. ________

7 Ben is holding a camera and a book. ________

Talk **Who does Grandpa want the children to meet? Tell a friend your ideas.**

Activities for pages 34–35

PET

1 Decide if the sentences are *correct* (A) or *incorrect* (B).

1 Ben and Rosie recognized the man sitting inside. A B

2 The man had gray hair and lines on his face. A B

3 Tom had waited a short time to see Ben and Rosie again. A B

4 When Tom and Mike came home, nobody talked to them. A B

5 Professor Muller asked Tom and Mike not to tell anyone about what happened. A B

6 Tom gave Ben his baseball. A B

7 Alice saw a photo of Grandpa when he was young. A B

8 In the photo, Grandpa was with Tom and Mike. A B

9 Grandpa was Richard. A B

10 Grandpa couldn't go on the trip because he didn't want to see Tom and Mike. A B

2 Who said this? Write the names.

1 'I've waited many years to see you again.' ____________

2 'Were you the teenager who helped us?' ____________

3 'The Moon's beautiful this evening.' ____________

Talk **Why do you like this story? Talk to a friend.**

Project

A Space Adventure

1 You are going to write a space adventure. First, think about some useful space vocabulary for your story. Using your own words, write the meaning of these words from *The Secret of the Moon*.

the Moon ______________________

gravity ______________________

astronaut ______________________

space ______________________

crater ______________________

spacesuit ______________________

orbit ______________________

landing vehicle ______________________

2 Now do some research to find some more useful space vocabulary. Write the words and their meanings.

Talk Compare your words with a friend's words. Are they similar or quite different?

3 Write some notes to plan your space adventure.

Where –

When –

Characters (people) –

Plot (what happens) –

Ending –

4 Now write your story.

____

____

____

____

____

____

____

____

____

____

____

____

____

____

____

Talk Read your space adventure to a friend.

Glossary

Here are some words used in this book, and you can check what they mean. Use a dictionary to check other new words.

appear *verb*
to suddenly be seen

astronaut *noun*
a person who works and travels in space

breathe *verb*
to take in and let out air through your nose and mouth

confused *adjective*
not able to think clearly

darkness *noun*
when there is no light

die *verb*
to stop living

disappear *verb*
when something goes away so people cannot see it

dust *noun*
dry dirt that is like powder

Earth *noun*
this world; the planet we live on

film *verb*
to use a camera to make a video

first *noun, pronoun*
a person or thing that comes earliest or before all others

good luck *noun*
success brought by chance rather than through your own actions

gravity *noun*
the force that pulls everything towards the Earth

head *noun*
the person in charge of a group of people or an organization

helmet *noun*
a hard hat that keeps your head safe

knock *verb*
to hit something and make a noise

ladder *noun*
a thing that you climb up when you want to get to a high place

land *verb*
to come down onto the ground from the air

landing *noun*
coming down onto the ground in a plane or space vehicle

live *adjective*
if something is live, you see or hear it at the same time as it happens

low *adjective*
near the ground

million *number*
1,000,000; one thousand thousand

notice *verb*
to see or pay attention to someone or something

orbit *verb*
to move around something in space

part *noun*
some, but not all, of something; one of the pieces of something

proud *adjective*
pleased about something that you or others have done or about something that you have

real *adjective*
existing; not imagined

recognize *verb*
to know again someone or something that you have seen or heard before

record *verb*
to save music or video using an electronic device, so that you can listen or watch later

satellite *noun*
a piece of electronic equipment that people send into space

scary *adjective*
making you feel afraid

shed *noun*
a small building where you keep things

signal *noun*
a light, sound or movement that tells you something without words

spacesuit *noun*
special clothes worn by astronauts in space

surface *noun*
the outside part of something

take off *verb*
when a plane or rocket leaves the ground and starts to fly

teenager *noun*
a person who is between 13 and 19 years old

telescope *noun*
a long, round piece of equipment with special glass inside it which makes things that are far away appear bigger

thought *noun*
an idea

train *verb*
to teach a person or animal to do something

trouble *noun*
a difficulty or problem

tunnel *noun*
a long hole under the ground or ocean for a road or railroad

unconscious *adjective*
if you are unconscious, you are in a kind of sleep and you do not know what is happening

vehicle *noun*
a car, bus, truck, bicycle, etc.; a thing that takes people or things from place to place

worry *verb*
to feel that something bad will happen or has already happened

Definitions in this glossary are taken and adapted from Oxford American Dictionaries for learners of English

Oxford Read and Imagine

Oxford Read and Imagine graded readers are at nine levels (Early Starter, Starter, Beginner, and Levels 1 to 6) for students from age 3 or 4 and older. They offer great stories to read and enjoy.

Activities provide Cambridge Young Learners Exams preparation. See Key below.

At Levels 1 to 6, every storybook reader links to an **Oxford Read and Discover** non-fiction reader, giving students a chance to find out more about the world around them, and an opportunity for Content and Language Integrated Learning (CLIL).

For more information about **Read and Imagine**, and for Teacher's Notes, go to www.oup.com/elt/teacher/readandimagine

KEY

- KET Activity supports Cambridge Key English Test Exam preparation
- PET Activity supports Cambridge Preliminary English Test Exam preparation

Oxford Read and Discover

When did the first person walk on the Moon? To find out, and to discover more about our galaxy and everything in the universe, you can read this non-fiction book.

OXFORD
UNIVERSITY PRESS

Great Clarendon Street, Oxford, OX2 6DP, United Kingdom

Oxford University Press is a department of the University of Oxford. It furthers the University's objective of excellence in research, scholarship,and education by publishing worldwide. Oxford is a registered trade mark of Oxford University Press in the UK and in certain other countries

First published in 2015
2019 2018 2017 2016 2015
10 9 8 7 6 5 4 3 2 1

ISBN: 978 0 19 472385 5

Printed in China

This book is printed on paper from certified and well-managed sources

ACKNOWLEDGEMENTS

Main illustrations by: Carl Pearce/Advocate Art